GAME DAY: FOOTBALL

DEFENSIVE BACKS

By Jim Gigliotti

Reading consultant: Cecilia Minden-Cupp, Ph.D.,
Literacy Specialist

Gareth Stevens
Publishing

Please visit our web site at www.garethstevens.com.
For a free catalog describing Gareth Stevens Publishing's list of high-quality books, call 1-800-542-2595 (USA) or 1-800-387-3178 (Canada). Gareth Stevens Publishing's fax: 1-877-542-2596

Library of Congress Cataloging-in-Publication Data
Gigliotti, Jim.
  Defensive backs / by Jim Gigliotti.
    p. cm. — (Game day. Football)
    Includes bibliographical references and index.
    ISBN-10: 1-4339-1964-8 — ISBN-13: 978-1-4339-1964-0 (lib. bdg.)
    1. Defensive backs (Football) —United States—Juvenile literature.
    2. Defensive backs (Football)—United States—Biography—Juvenile literature. I. Title.
GV951.18.G53   2009
796.332'24—dc22   2009006801

This edition first published in 2010 by
Gareth Stevens Publishing
A Weekly Reader® Company
1 Reader's Digest Road
Pleasantville, NY 10570-7000 USA

Copyright © 2010 by Gareth Stevens, Inc.

Executive Managing Editor: Lisa M. Herrington
Senior Editor: Brian Fitzgerald
Senior Designer: Keith Plechaty

Produced by Q2AMedia
Art Direction: Rahul Dhiman
Senior Designer: Dibakar Acharjee
Image Researcher: Kamal Kumar

Photo credits
Key: t = top, b = bottom, c = center, l = left, r = right
Cover and title page: Gregory Shamus/Getty Images.
George Gojkovich/Getty Images: 4; Rob Tringali/Sportschrome/Getty Images: 5; Pro Football Hall of Fame/NFL: 6; Pro Football Hall of Fame/Getty Images: 7; Pro Football Hall of Fame/NFL: 8; Nate Fine/NFL: 9; Pro Football Hall of Fame/NFL: 10; NFL/Getty Images: 11; George Gojkovich/Getty Images: 12bl; Tony Tomsic/NFL: 12tr; George Rose/Getty Images: 13; George Gojkovich/Getty Images: 14; Mitchell Layton/Getty Images: 15; Scott Boehm/Getty Images: 17, 18; Joe Robbins/Getty Images: 19; Greg Trott/Getty Images: 20; Tom Hauck/Getty Images: 21; Larry French/Getty Images: 22; Rob Tringali/Sportschrome/Getty Images: 23; Tom Hauck/Getty Images: 24; Joe Robbins/Getty Images: 25; Greg Trott/Getty Images: 26; Mike Ehrmann/NFL: 27; Greg Trott/Getty Images: 28; Wesley Hitt/Getty Images: 29; Tom Hauck/Getty Images: 30; Jed Jacobsohn/Getty Images: 31; Stephen Dunn/Getty Images: 32; Joe Robbins/Getty Images: 34; Al Bello/Getty Images: 35; Greg Trott/Getty Images: 36; Hunter Martin/Getty Images: 37; Joe Robbins/Getty Images: 38; Jim McIsaac/Getty Images: 39; Mike Eliason: 40, 41, 42, 43; George Gojkovich/Getty Images: 44; Tony Tomsic/NFL: 45.
Q2AMedia Art Bank: 16, 33.

All rights reserved. No part of this book may be reproduced, stored in a retrieval system, or transmitted in any form or by any means, electronic, mechanical, photocopying, recording, or otherwise, without the prior written permission of the copyright holder. For permission, contact **permissions@gspub.com**.

Printed in the United States of America

CPSIA Compliance Information: Batch#CR909011GS: For further information contact Gareth Stevens, New York, New York at 1-800-542-2595

Cover: Troy Polamalu of the Pittsburgh Steelers is one of the top defensive backs in pro football.

Contents

The Last Line of Defense 4

Chapter 1: Birth of the Defensive Backs ... 6

Chapter 2: The Early Stars 10

Chapter 3: How to Play DB 16

Chapter 4: Stars of Today 34

Chapter 5: Future Star: You! 40

Record Book 44

Glossary 46

Find Out More 47

Index 48

Words in the glossary appear in **bold** type the first time they are used in the text.

The Last Line of Defense

The defensive backs, or DBs, are the cornerbacks and the safeties on a football team. They are the last line of defense. If a ball carrier or pass catcher gets behind the DBs, watch out! It's a sure touchdown for the offense.

BIG PLAY

On January 18, 2009, the Pittsburgh Steelers led the Baltimore Ravens 16–14 in the fourth quarter. The winner would go to the Super Bowl. The Ravens were driving toward a possible go-ahead score. Ravens quarterback Joe Flacco dropped back to pass. He looked to his right. He tried to throw over Pittsburgh safety Troy Polamalu to reach his receiver. Bad move! Polamalu leaped and made a perfect **interception**.

▶ After intercepting Joe Flacco's pass, Troy Polamalu runs for the end zone.

POLAMALU TO THE RESCUE

Polamalu charged down the field. He cut to his right and ran all the way across the field. He followed the blocks by his teammates. A few seconds later, he churned into the end zone. Touchdown, Steelers! The score clinched a spot in Super Bowl XLIII for Pittsburgh. The Steelers won that game, too!

Defensive backs make many big plays during every NFL game. Read on to learn more about these fast and fierce defenders.

◀ Troy Polamalu celebrates after his big interception return for a touchdown.

GLOSSARY

interception: a pass that is caught by the defense

CHAPTER 1

Birth of the Defensive Backs

Football in its early days was very different than the modern game. All the action took place along the **line of scrimmage**. There were no defensive backs. Passing was not even allowed!

EARLY FOOTBALL GAMES

You might have heard the expression "Three yards and a cloud of dust." That's what early football games were like. The fields often were dirt with little grass. Teams ran the ball straight ahead. Each play was a giant collision of players on offense and defense. Games were not very exciting for fans.

▼ The first defensive halfbacks had to tackle runners more often than they stopped receivers.

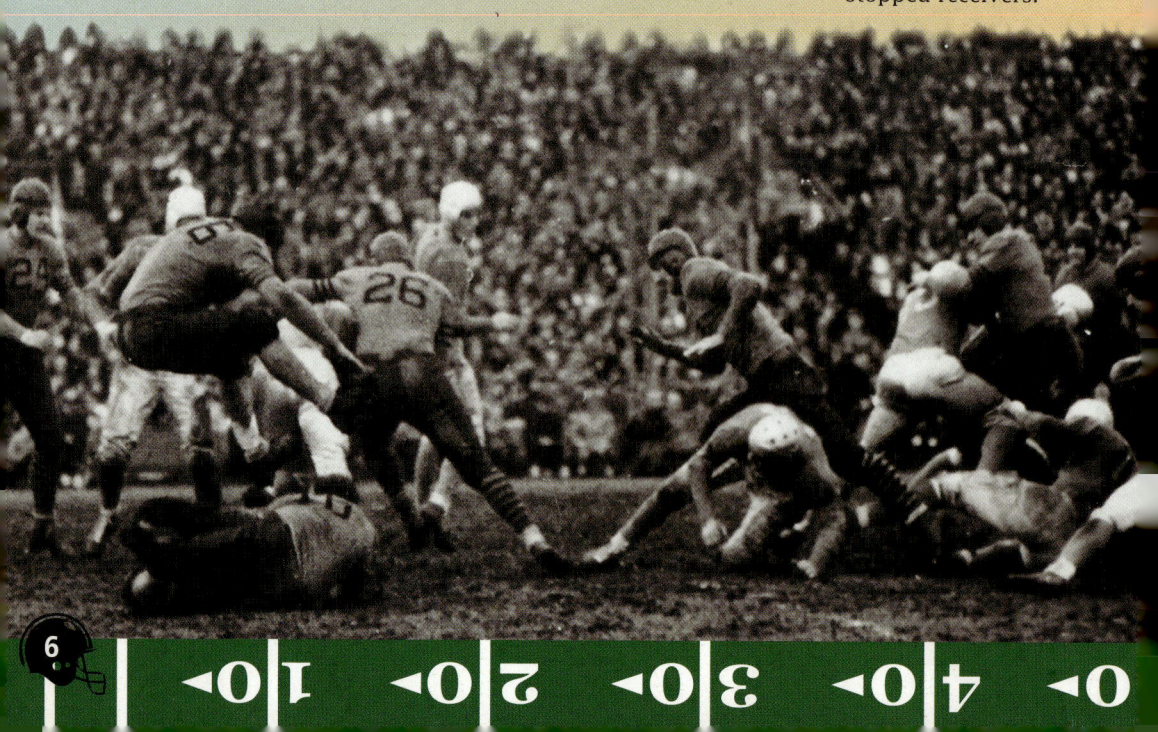

THE GAME CHANGES

The forward pass was legalized in 1906. It took many years for passing to "catch" on. Eventually, coaches figured out ways to use passes effectively. Defenses had to adjust. Teams needed players who could defend against the pass. Players needed to cover more of the field. The position of defensive back was born. These players were often called "defensive halfbacks."

◀ Sid Luckman (42) of the Chicago Bears was one of the first great pro quarterbacks. Teams needed good defensive backs to try to stop the passing game.

GLOSSARY

line of scrimmage: the imaginary line that divides the offense and the defense before each play

▶ Don Hutson of the Green Bay Packers was the best receiver in the NFL in the 1930s. He was also a terrific defensive back.

NO SUBS

The National Football League (NFL) formed in 1920. In the early days of the league, teams were not allowed to substitute players whenever they wanted. Players lined up on both offense and defense. They were called "two-way" players. Defensive backs usually were the same men who played quarterback or running back on offense. That made sense. They were used to handling the ball, and they were often the fastest players.

Two Positions

There are two types of defensive backs. Cornerbacks start close to the line of scrimmage. They cover receivers who run down the field. Safeties start farther away from the line. They help cover receivers or charge up to tackle ball carriers.

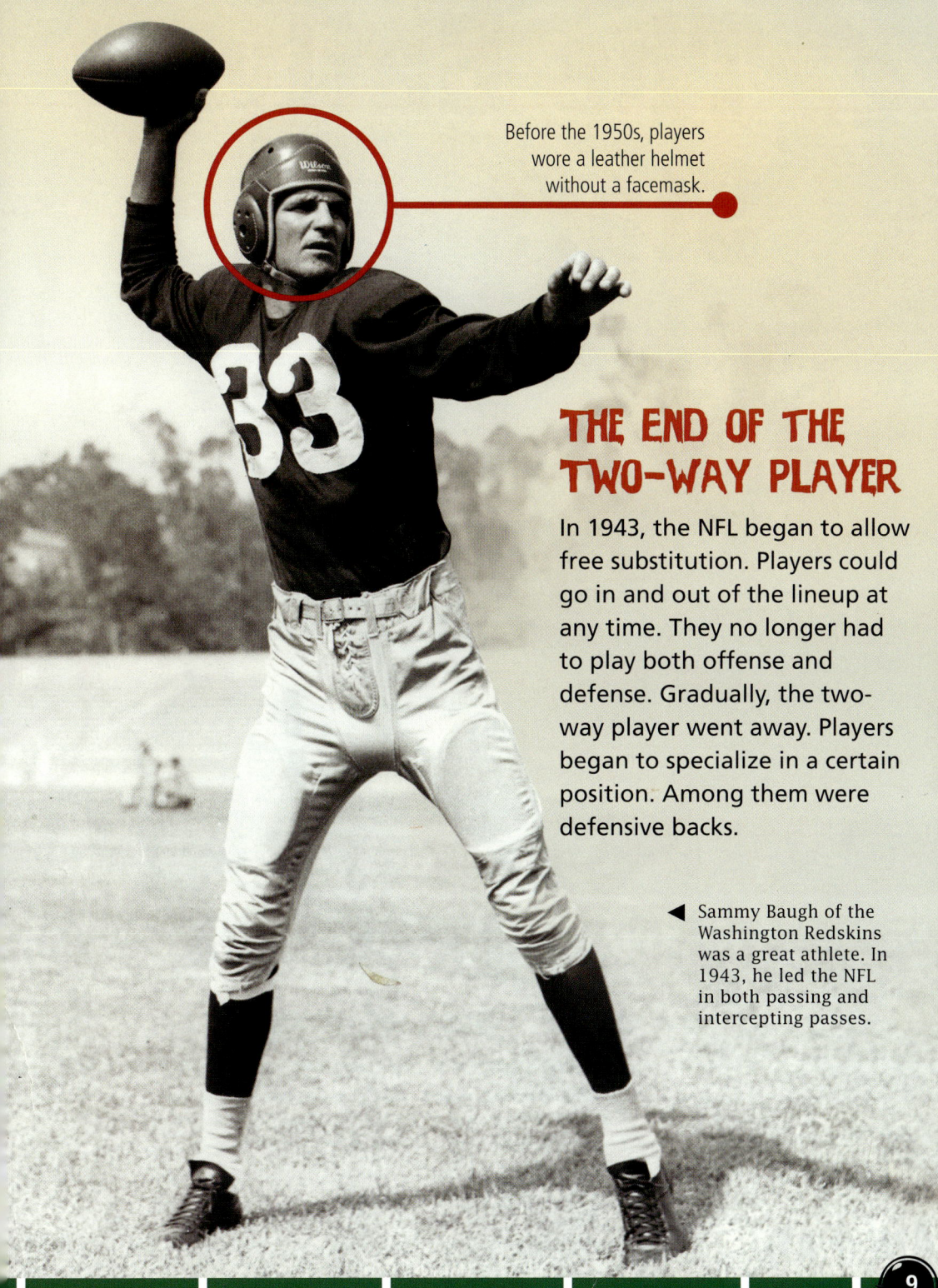

Before the 1950s, players wore a leather helmet without a facemask.

THE END OF THE TWO-WAY PLAYER

In 1943, the NFL began to allow free substitution. Players could go in and out of the lineup at any time. They no longer had to play both offense and defense. Gradually, the two-way player went away. Players began to specialize in a certain position. Among them were defensive backs.

◀ Sammy Baugh of the Washington Redskins was a great athlete. In 1943, he led the NFL in both passing and intercepting passes.

CHAPTER 2

The Early Stars

Let's meet some of the star defensive backs of the past.

UMBRELLA MAN

In the 1950s, the New York Giants had a creative defense. It was called "the Umbrella Defense" because the defensive backs lined up in a giant, open-umbrella shape. Safety Emlen Tunnell was the man who made that defense work so well. Sportswriters called him New York's "offense on defense." Tunnell had 79 interceptions in his 14-year career.

▶ Emlen Tunnell (45, in front) uses his height to reach up and knock away a pass.

NIGHT TRAIN

Dick "Night Train" Lane joined the Los Angeles Rams as a wide receiver in 1952. The Rams already had a couple of terrific pass catchers, though. So they moved Lane to cornerback on defense. What a great decision! Lane intercepted 14 passes as a **rookie** that year. That's still the most ever by an NFL player in one season.

GLOSSARY

rookie: a player in his first season of pro football

HE'S NUMBER ONE

Paul Krause intercepted 12 passes for the Washington Redskins as a rookie in 1964. The young safety was just getting warmed up. After three more seasons in Washington, Krause played 12 years for the Minnesota Vikings. He holds the NFL record for most career interceptions. He finished with 81 interceptions in 16 seasons.

▼ Paul Krause was a strong, steady player with a nose for the football.

Star Steeler

Pittsburgh had a famous defense in the 1970s. It was called "the Steel Curtain." The Steel Curtain helped Pittsburgh win four Super Bowls in six years. Cornerback Mel Blount was one of several players on that defense who made the **Pro Football Hall of Fame**. He often lined up against the other team's best wide receiver—and shut him down!

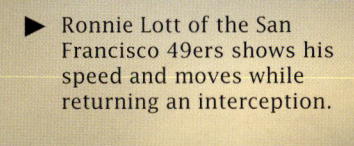

▶ Ronnie Lott of the San Francisco 49ers shows his speed and moves while returning an interception.

BIG HITTER

Ronnie Lott played defensive back like he was a linebacker. In other words, he was rugged, tough, and loved to make big hits on receivers. Lott intercepted 63 passes in his 14-year career. He also made more than 1,000 tackles. Lott began as a cornerback in 1981 and made the **Pro Bowl**. A few years later, the 49ers moved him to safety. He made the Pro Bowl there, too.

GLOSSARY

Pro Football Hall of Fame: a museum in Canton, Ohio, that honors football's greatest stars

Pro Bowl: the NFL's annual all-star game

Superman

Rod Woodson once posed for a magazine cover in a Superman outfit. Why? Because he could do just about anything on a football field. In college, he played offense and defense and returned kicks. The Pittsburgh Steelers **drafted** him in 1987. They didn't use him on offense. He was too valuable on defense and as a return man. Woodson is the only player to earn Pro Bowls selections as a kick returner, safety, and cornerback.

▶ Rod Woodson causes a fumble with a big hit on a quarterback.

GLOSSARY

drafted: selected from the top college football players

sprinter: a track-and-field athlete who runs very fast over short distances

SPRINTER'S SPEED

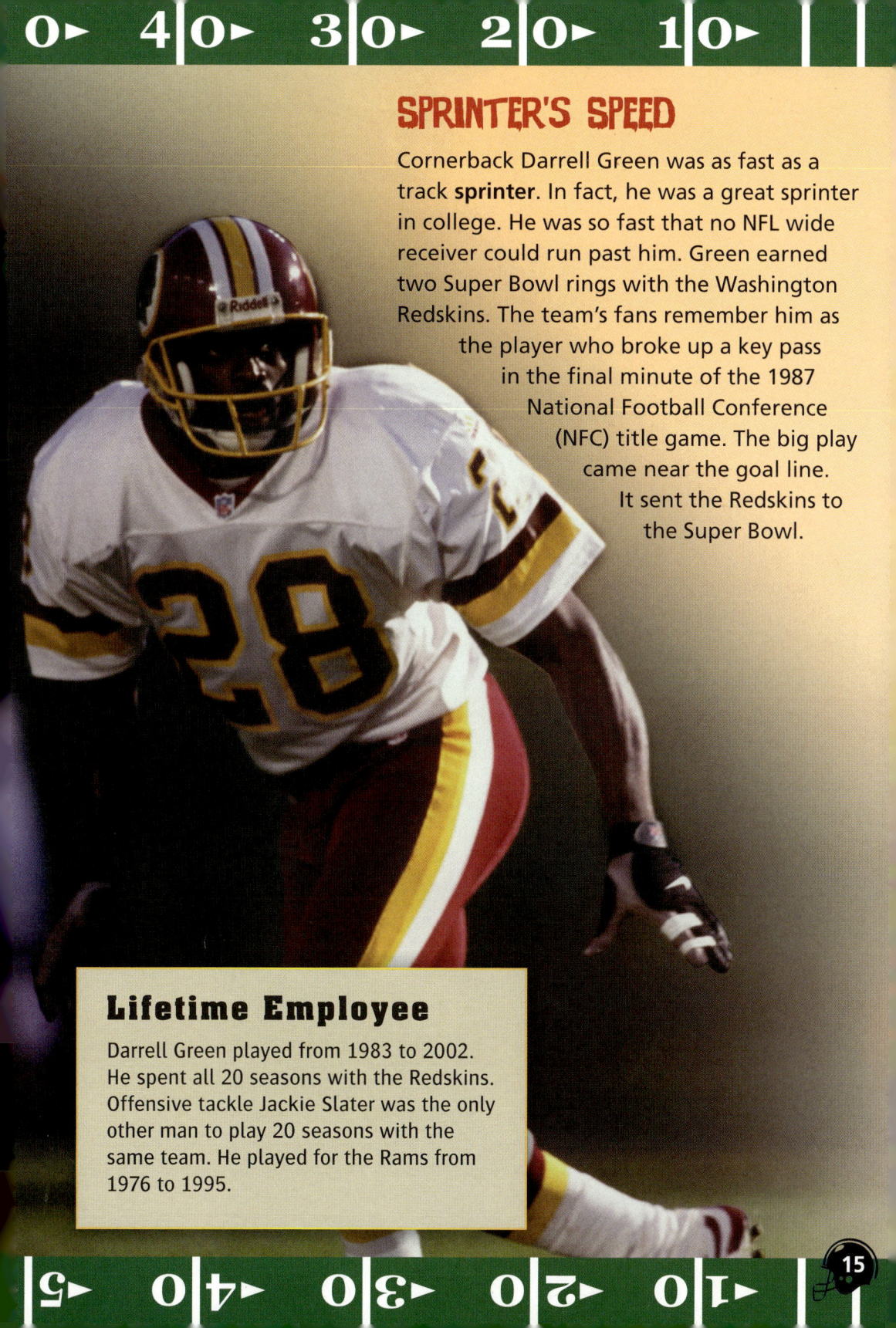

Cornerback Darrell Green was as fast as a track **sprinter**. In fact, he was a great sprinter in college. He was so fast that no NFL wide receiver could run past him. Green earned two Super Bowl rings with the Washington Redskins. The team's fans remember him as the player who broke up a key pass in the final minute of the 1987 National Football Conference (NFC) title game. The big play came near the goal line. It sent the Redskins to the Super Bowl.

Lifetime Employee

Darrell Green played from 1983 to 2002. He spent all 20 seasons with the Redskins. Offensive tackle Jackie Slater was the only other man to play 20 seasons with the same team. He played for the Rams from 1976 to 1995.

CHAPTER 3

How to Play DB

Covering receivers takes skills such as speed and strength. Knowing where to play is just as important. Here's a look at everything a defensive back needs to know.

THE BASICS

Most teams use four defensive backs at a time. A pair of cornerbacks line up opposite the offensive team's two wide receivers. Defenses usually have a right cornerback and a left cornerback. Sometimes, though, a cornerback is assigned to cover a particular wide receiver. Two safeties set up behind the cornerbacks. Together, all the defensive backs make up the defensive backfield, or secondary.

Defensive Positions

FS   SS

CB   OLB   ILB   ILB   OLB   CB

DE   NT   DE

Key
DE: Defensive end
NT: Nose tackle
OLB: Outside linebacker
ILB: Inside linebacker
CB: Cornerback
FS: Free safety
SS: Strong safety

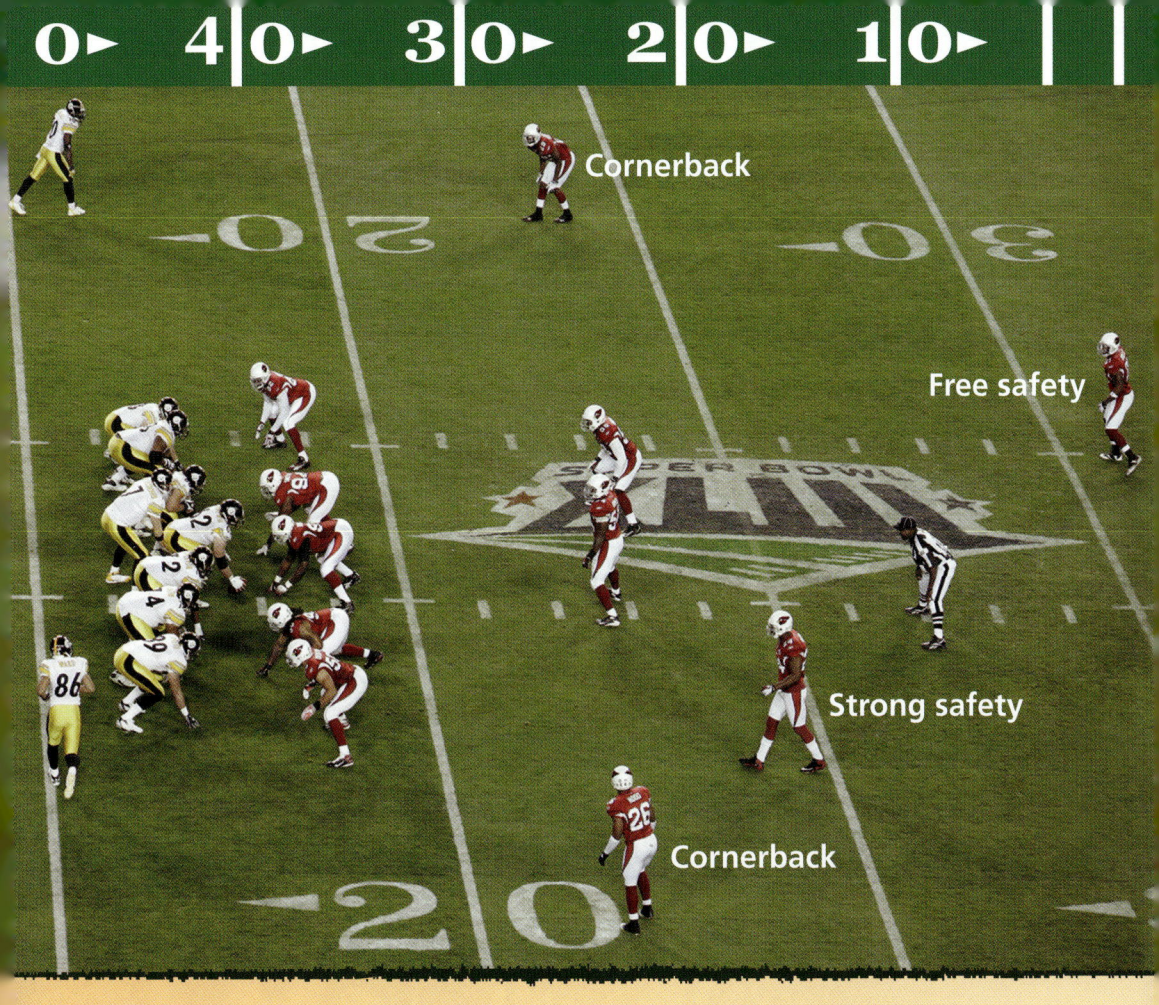

▲ The Arizona Cardinals secondary awaits the next play during Super Bowl XLIII.

STRONG AND FREE

Most teams use two types of safeties. The strong safety lines up on the same side of the field as the tight end does on offense. That is called the strong side of the offense. The free safety lines up on the other side. He usually stands several yards deeper than the strong safety. He is "free" to move to wherever the defense needs extra help.

Nickel and Dime

Sometimes, the defense figures the other team is going to pass. It sends in an extra defensive back. That player is called the "nickel back" because he's the fifth DB. A second extra defensive back is called the "dime back." Why? Two nickels equal one dime!

Types of Defenses

Teams play two basic types of defense: zone and man-for-man. Defensive backs must know how to play both equally well.

MAN-FOR-MAN

In man-for-man coverage, a cornerback is assigned to cover a specific wide receiver. The cornerback goes wherever the wide receiver goes. The strong safety usually covers the offense's tight end. He may cover a third wide receiver instead. The free safety is usually still "free" to go wherever he is needed most.

▼ Cornerback Darrelle Revis (24) of the New York Jets plays man-for-man against Wes Welker of the New England Patriots.

▼ Safeties Michael Griffin (33) and Chris Hope (24) of the Tennessee Titans keep their eyes on the quarterback as they drop back into pass coverage.

IN THE ZONE

In zone coverage, defensive backs are assigned a specific area of the field. They are responsible for defending any pass that comes into that area. Different zones include areas such as middle, outside, deep middle, deep half, and deep outside.

BUMP-AND-RUN

In man-for-man coverage, cornerbacks play bump-and-run. DBs can bump the wide receiver within five yards of the line of scrimmage as long as the ball hasn't been thrown. Some cornerbacks like bump-and-run defense because it allows them to be aggressive. Bumping a receiver can knock him off his **route**, or pattern. A bump can also disrupt the timing between the quarterback and receiver.

Neion Deion

Deion Sanders was one of the best ever at man-for-man coverage. He used his quick feet and outstanding speed to stick with any receiver. He got so good that teams would rarely throw the ball toward a receiver he was covering.

▼ Defensive back Michael Huff of the Oakland Raiders "bumps" receiver Andre Johnson of the Houston Texans.

GLOSSARY

route: the path a receiver takes as he goes out for a pass

Ralph Brown (20) of the Cardinals turns to run with receiver Steve Smith (89) of the Carolina Panthers.

TURN-AND-RUN

In either man-for-man or zone, cornerbacks can give the wide receiver a "cushion." They might be willing to give up a short pass completion. Or they might be worried that the receiver will sprint past them for a **bomb**. Using turn-and-run, they are ready for either. They can attack when the pass is thrown short, or they can turn and run down the field.

GLOSSARY

bomb: a long, high pass that often leads to a touchdown

FIELD VISION

No matter what type of defense their team is using, DBs have to be aware of what is going on all over the field. They have to worry about more than just what is right in front of them. They need to know when it's time to leave their man and help out with a tackle. Covering the receiver is the main job. If the pass doesn't come their way, they still have work to do.

▲ In pass coverage, Antoine Winfield of the Minnesota Vikings watches the quarterback. He also has to look out for receivers who come into his zone.

Troy Polamalu drops into pass coverage after deciding that the play is a pass.

RUN OR PASS?

On every play, defensive backs have to quickly determine if it is a run or a pass. Sounds easy, right? Well, the quarterback might try to trick the secondary with a **play-action pass**. That's when the quarterback fakes a handoff to a running back and then throws a pass. If a defensive back is faked out, a receiver might go right past him.

GLOSSARY

play-action pass: an offensive play in which the quarterback fakes a handoff before making a pass

Key Skills

In any defense or formation, defensive backs need to have certain skills. Here are the ABCs of DBs.

SETTING UP

It's important for a DB to start a play in the proper stance. If he doesn't, the receiver might beat him for a long pass. Cornerbacks lean forward at the waist. Their feet are as wide apart as the shoulders. Their arms hang loose at the sides. The outside foot (the one closest to the sideline) is slightly forward. Safeties start much the same way. They are more upright, however.

Most DBs wear gloves to help them catch passes.

▶ Terence Newman of the Dallas Cowboys shows excellent starting form for a cornerback.

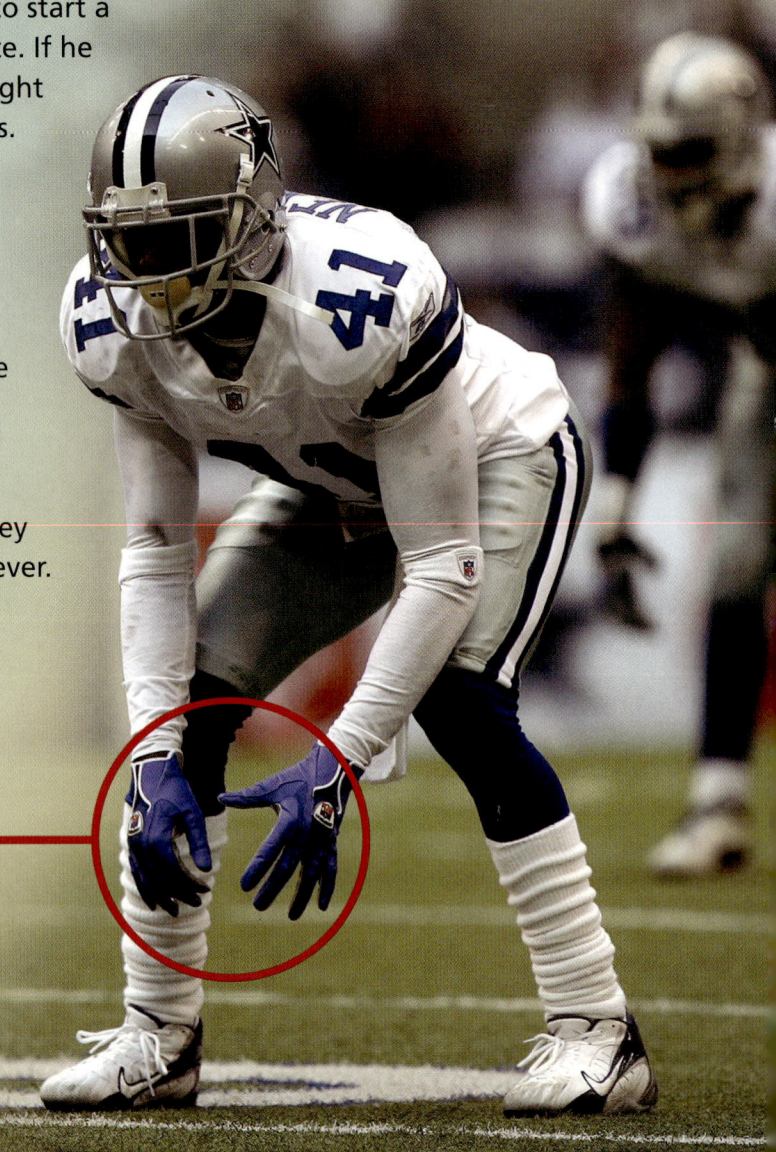

MOVING BACK . . . FAST!

When the ball is snapped, the receiver runs forward. The DB runs backward! The DB backpedals while still keeping an eye on the quarterback or the receiver. The DB doesn't just shuffle backward. He has to lift his feet and step backward. He also has to be ready to turn and run if necessary.

▲ Antonio Cromartie (31) of the San Diego Chargers begins to backpedal as the receiver he is covering starts to run forward.

THE NEED FOR SPEED

Almost all defensive backs are fast. Cornerbacks are some of the fastest players in all of sports. They have to be able cover speedy receivers who have one big advantage: The receiver knows where he is going! All DBs need the speed to chase down the quickest running backs. DBs also have to race from one side of the field to the other to help out other defenders.

▼ Cornerback Nnamdi Asomugha (21) of the Raiders has to keep up with speedy receivers. Steve Smith of the Carolina Panthers (89) is one of the fastest!

TIME TO LEAP

Many times, DBs are smaller than the receivers they are covering. DBs often have to jump very high at just the right time. If a DB gets to the ball too late, the receiver may be gone for a touchdown. If a DB gets there too early, he may get a penalty for pass interference. If he gets to the ball at just the right time, the pass is knocked away—or, even better, intercepted!

▲ Champ Bailey (24) of the Denver Broncos times his jump perfectly. He knocks the ball away from the receiver.

Move On

No matter how good they are, all defensive backs will get beat for touchdowns. They can't dwell on a mistake, though. They can't let it scare them into another bad play. Instead, they have to learn from their mistake and come back better next time.

Picked Off!

Once the play begins, the DB looks for the ball. A defensive back loves nothing more than making an interception. "Picking off" a pass can often turn a game around.

CAT AND MOUSE

A defensive back often makes an interception by "reading" the quarterback's eyes. That is, he sees where the quarterback intends to throw the ball. Then the DB "jumps" the wide receiver's route. He gets to the ball before the pass catcher does.

▶ Got it! Nnamdi Asomugha of the Raiders steps in front of a receiver to make an interception.

CATCHING THE BALL

The best defensive backs catch the ball as well as wide receivers do. The position of a pass catcher's hands depends on where the ball is thrown. He tries to make a basket with his hands. If the ball is at or above the chest, each of his thumbs and his index fingers should be touching. If the pass is below the chest area, his pinky fingers should be touching to create a different basket area. A DB doesn't always try to catch the ball, though. Many times, he simply tries to knock it down so the receiver can't catch it.

Pass catchers keep their hands away from their body. A ball that hits a player in the chest first will likely bounce away.

▶ Ronde Barber of the Tampa Bay Buccaneers shows good catching form on a high pass.

Run Support

Defensive backs do not just defend against passes, of course. They also tackle runners and **blitz** quarterbacks.

TACKLING

Remember, defensive backs are the last line of defense. On a running play, they can't allow a ball carrier to get past them. There is no one behind them to make tackles. It's important that DBs learn proper tackling technique. A tackler should always bend at the knees, not the waist. And it's very important that a tackler always keeps his head up. If he looks down at the ground, his neck could get injured.

▼ Charles Woodson (21) of the Green Bay Packers shows good tackling form. He stays low, keeps his head up, and wraps his arms around the runner's lower body.

HERE COMES THE BLITZ!

A blitz is when more than four players rush the quarterback. Usually, an extra rusher is a linebacker. But sometimes, it can be a DB. A blitz is usually a surprise for the offense. When it's timed just right, a blitz may result in a big **sack** and maybe a fumble.

▼ Sack! Safety Adrian Wilson of the Arizona Cardinals crashes into quarterback Donovan McNabb of the Philadelphia Eagles.

When making tackles, defenders often try to strip, or pull, the ball away from the ball carrier.

GLOSSARY

blitz: a rush of the quarterback by linebackers or defensive backs

sack: a tackle of the quarterback behind the line of scrimmage

Study Time

A defensive back's work begins long before game day. Classroom work, film study, and practice are all in a day's work for an NFL cornerback or safety.

PRACTICE, PRACTICE, PRACTICE

Defensive backs cover their own team's receivers in practice. They get to see the receivers' moves and learn how to stop them. The more moves and fakes that a defensive back sees, the better chance he'll have of stopping the opponent. Most teams have passing-game practice at least twice a week before each game.

▼ Dallas cornerback Terence Newman (41) improves his skills by covering a teammate in practice.

THE PASSING TREE

All DBs learn about the **passing tree**. The passing tree includes all the routes that a receiver might run. All teams use the same basic passing tree. The names of the routes might just be a little different. Knowing the routes that receivers will run in a game helps a defensive back prepare to stop them.

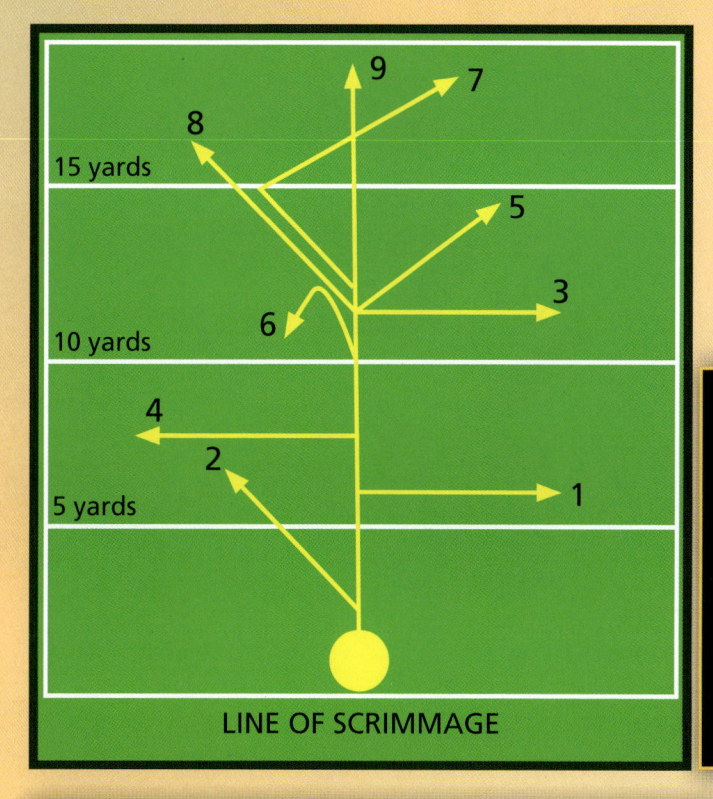

Key
1: Quick Out
2: Slant
3: Deep Out
4: Drag / In
5: Flag
6: Curl
7: Post Corner
8: Post
9: Fly

Film School

A good DB watches a lot of film of the team he is about to play against. He learns when the opponent likes to pass and likes to run. He studies the wide receivers, too. He learns what routes they like best. By the time Sunday comes, the DB is prepared for whatever might come his way.

GLOSSARY

passing tree: a diagram that shows different routes, or patterns, that a receiver runs

CHAPTER 4

Stars of Today

Let's take a look at some of the NFL's top defensive backs.

THE PLAYMAKER

Darren Sharper is a playmaker on defense. Opposing quarterbacks have to know where the Minnesota Vikings safety is on every play. Sharper entered the 2009 season with 54 career interceptions. He returned those picks an amazing 1,036 yards! He scored eight times on interception returns, too.

▶ Darren Sharper sets his sights on a ball carrier.

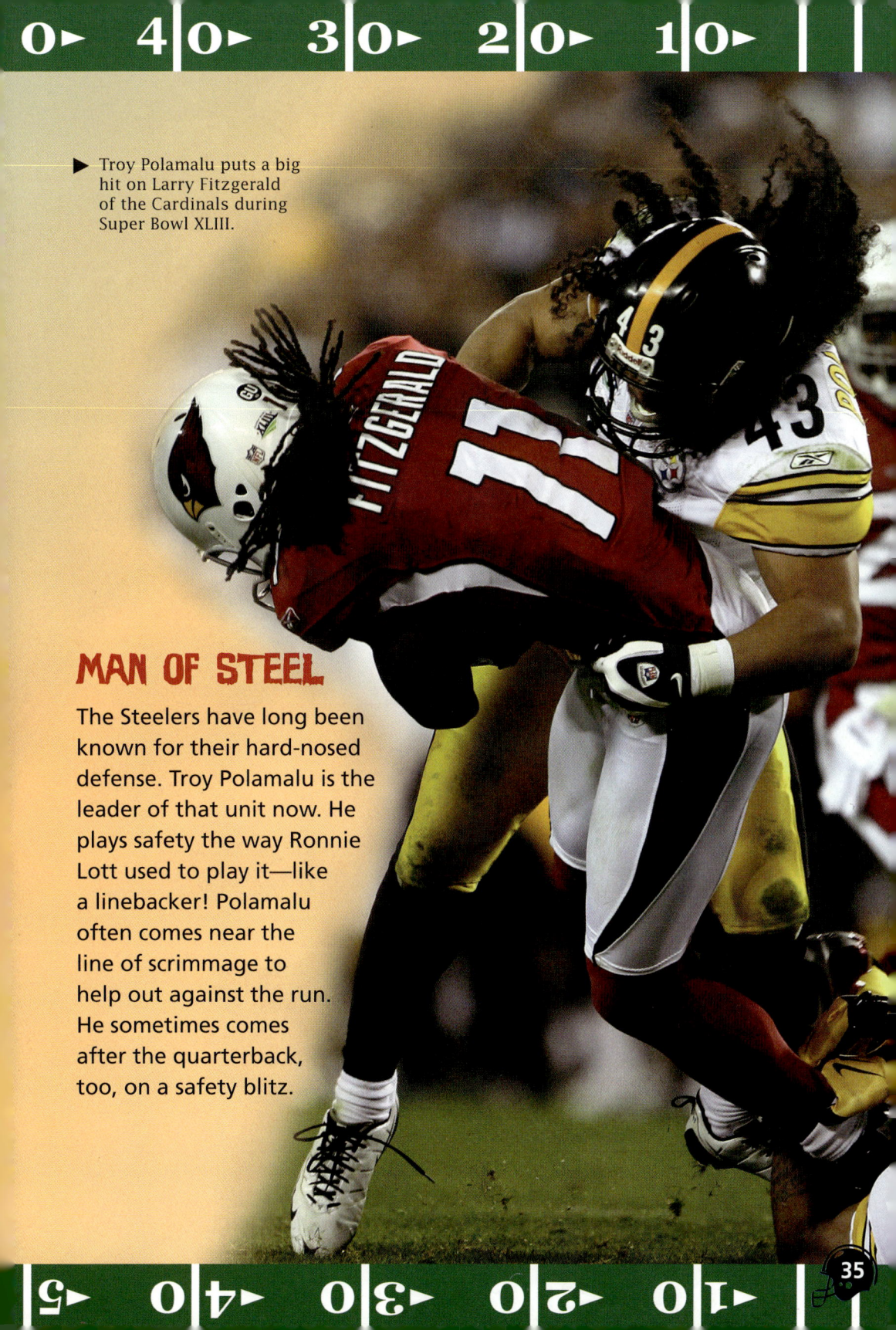

▶ Troy Polamalu puts a big hit on Larry Fitzgerald of the Cardinals during Super Bowl XLIII.

MAN OF STEEL

The Steelers have long been known for their hard-nosed defense. Troy Polamalu is the leader of that unit now. He plays safety the way Ronnie Lott used to play it—like a linebacker! Polamalu often comes near the line of scrimmage to help out against the run. He sometimes comes after the quarterback, too, on a safety blitz.

THE CHAMP

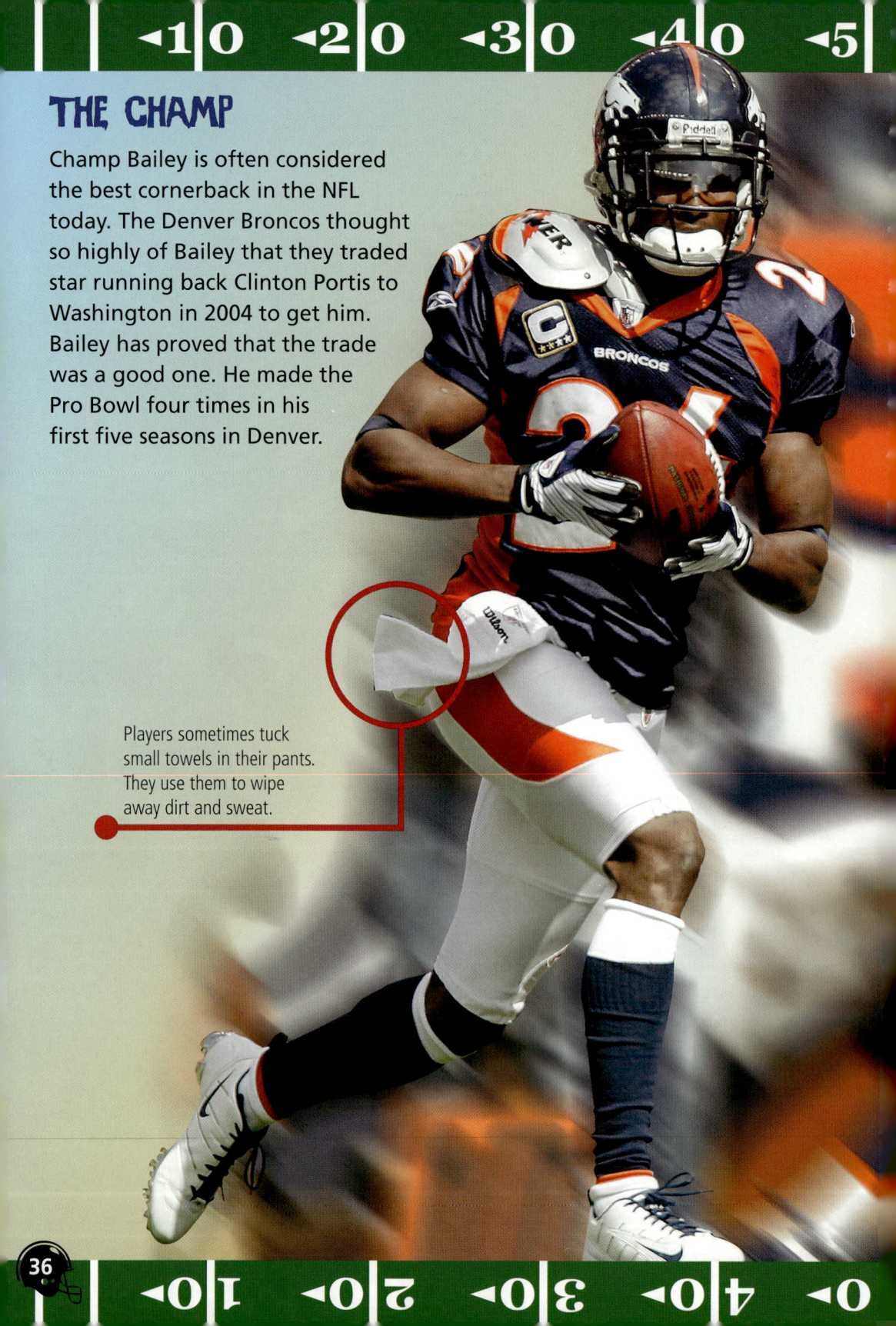

Champ Bailey is often considered the best cornerback in the NFL today. The Denver Broncos thought so highly of Bailey that they traded star running back Clinton Portis to Washington in 2004 to get him. Bailey has proved that the trade was a good one. He made the Pro Bowl four times in his first five seasons in Denver.

Players sometimes tuck small towels in their pants. They use them to wipe away dirt and sweat.

FREE-AGENT GEM

The Philadelphia Eagles signed Asante Samuel to a big contract as a **free agent** in 2008. They knew the talented cornerback was a winner. Samuel had helped the New England Patriots win a couple of Super Bowls. He intercepted a pass in 17 regular-season games for the Patriots. New England won every one of them!

GLOSSARY

free agent: a player who has completed his contract with one team and is "free" to sign with any other team

TOP HONOR

Every football fan knows about the Indianapolis Colts offense. Quarterback Peyton Manning and his teammates grab most of the headlines. But the Colts didn't win the Super Bowl until they got a good defense, too. In 2007, safety Bob Sanders became the first player in club history to be named NFL Defensive Player of the Year. Sanders is only 5 feet 8 inches tall. That's not big for a football player. But Sanders is one of the toughest players and hardest hitters in the NFL.

SAFETY FIRST

It's easy to find safety Ed Reed when the Baltimore Ravens are on defense. Just look for the ball. Reed is sure to be close by! Reed intercepted 43 passes from 2002 to 2008. He led the NFL with nine picks in 2008. That year, he returned an interception against Philadelphia 107 yards for a touchdown. That was the longest interception return in NFL history.

◀ Ed Reed races toward the end zone during his record-setting interception return.

CHAPTER 5

Future Star: You!

Would you like to be a defensive back? Here are some good ways to practice important skills.

GET BACK!

Practice backpedaling, or running backward. Start in the stance shown on page 24. As you step backward, stay on your toes and keep your body bent forward slightly. Move your arms in a back-and-forth motion. Run backward in short spurts. Then try sprinting forward and moving side-to-side. A defensive back uses all of those skills—often on the same play.

QUICK START

DBs need to react quickly to the snap of the ball. If a DB is slow to react, the receiver will run right by him. Have one friend be the quarterback. Have another be the wide receiver. At the snap, start to backpedal as the receiver bursts off the line. Turn and run to stay alongside the receiver. The quarterback should change the **snap count** each time. That helps the defensive back focus and react quickly to the movement of the receiver and the ball.

Warning!

Don't try tackling until you have the proper safety equipment and are supervised by a coach. The football players you see on TV wear helmets and a lot of padding. They have also learned the proper way to tackle from a coach. This will keep you—and your friends—from getting hurt.

◀ Staying on his toes helps a DB react quickly if the receiver changes directions.

GLOSSARY

snap count: the words or numbers that a quarterback calls out to start each play

TIMING IS EVERYTHING

Breaking up passes is one of a DB's most important skills. Again, have two friends play quarterback and receiver. Work on stepping in front of the receiver to knock passes away. Remember not to push or touch the receiver, which would cause a penalty. The more you practice your timing, the better you'll get at preventing the receiver from making a catch.

Watch and See

The next-best thing to playing football is watching football. Go to a high school or college game near you. You can also check out games on TV. As you watch, pay special attention to the defensive backs. Watch how they cover the receivers. See how they react on running plays. You can learn a lot just by watching!

LET'S PLAY CATCH!

All defensive backs must catch the ball well. The best way to learn to catch well is by doing it—over and over again. Keep your eyes on the ball. Hold your hands away from your body. Remember to form a basket with your hands as you catch high or low throws. Try to have the point of the ball land in that basket.

Record Book

Who's the best of the best? Here are the top DBs in some key categories.

Interceptions, Career
1. Paul Krause: 81
2. Emlen Tunnell: 79
3. Rod Woodson: 71
4. Night Train Lane: 68
5. Ken Riley: 65

Interceptions, Season
1. Night Train Lane: 14 (1952)
2. Dan Sandifer: 13 (1948)
   Spec Sanders: 13 (1950)
   Lester Hayes: 13 (1980)
5. Many players: 12
   (Last time: Mike Reinfeldt, 1979)

Interceptions, Game
1. Many players: 4
   (Most recent: Deltha O'Neal, 2001)

ROD WOODSON

* All records are through the 2008 season.

Interception Returns for Touchdowns, Career
1. Rod Woodson: 12
2. Ken Houston: 9
   Aeneas Williams: 9
   Deion Sanders: 9
5. Eric Allen: 8
   Darren Sharper: 8

Interception Returns for Touchdowns, Season
1. Ken Houston: 4 (1971)
   Jim Kearney: 4 (1972)
   Eric Allen: 4 (1993)
4. Many players: 3
   (Most recent: Antrel Rolle, 2007)

Pro Bowl Selections
1. Ken Houston: 12
2. Rod Woodson: 11
3. Ronnie Lott: 10
   Mel Renfro: 10
5. Willie Brown: 9
   Mike Haynes: 9
   Yale Lary: 9
   John Lynch: 9
   Emlen Tunnell: 9

KEN HOUSTON

Glossary

blitz: a rush of the quarterback by linebackers or defensive backs

bomb: a long, high pass that often leads to a touchdown

drafted: selected from the top college football players

free agent: a player who has completed his contract with one team and is "free" to sign with any other team

interception: a pass that is caught by the defense

line of scrimmage: the imaginary line that divides the offense and the defense before each play

passing tree: a diagram that shows different routes, or patterns, that a receiver runs

play-action pass: an offensive play in which the quarterback fakes a handoff before making a pass

Pro Bowl: the NFL's annual all-star game

Pro Football Hall of Fame: a museum in Canton, Ohio, that honors football's greatest stars

rookie: a player in his first season of pro football

route: the path a receiver takes as he goes out for a pass

sack: a tackle of the quarterback behind the line of scrimmage

snap count: the words or numbers that a quarterback calls out to start each play

sprinter: a track-and-field athlete who runs very fast over short distances

Find Out More

Books

Buckley, James, Jr., Jim Gigliotti, Matt Marini, and John Wiebusch. *The Child's World Encyclopedia of the NFL*. Mankato, MN: The Child's World, 2008.

Pellowski, Michael J. *A Little Giant Book: Football Facts*. New York: Sterling Publishing, 2007.

Stewart, Mark. *The Ultimate 10: Football*. Pleasantville, N.Y.: Gareth Stevens, 2009.

Web Sites

www.nfl.com
The official web site of the National Football League is packed with stats, video, news, and player biographies. Football fans can find all they need to know about their favorite players and teams here.

www.nflrush.com
Check out the official kids' site of the NFL. Meet star players, see video of great plays, and get tips from the pros!

www.profootballhof.com
Find out more about the history of pro football and meet the legends of the game at the Pro Football Hall of Fame site.

Publisher's note to educators and parents: Our editors have carefully reviewed these web sites to ensure that they are suitable for children. Many web sites change frequently, however, and we cannot guarantee that a site's future contents will continue to meet our high standards of quality and educational value. Be advised that children should be closely supervised whenever they access the Internet.

Index

Arizona Cardinals 17, 20, 31, 35
Asomugha, Nnamdi 26, 28

Bailey, Champ 27, 36
Baltimore Ravens 4, 39
Barber, Ronde 29
Baugh, Sammy 9
Blount, Mel 12
Brown, Ralph 21

Carolina Panthers 21, 26
Chicago Bears 7
Cromartie, Antonio 25

Dallas Cowboys 24, 32
Denver Broncos 27, 36

Fitzgerald, Larry 35
Flacco, Joe 4

Green Bay Packers 8, 10, 30
Green, Darrell 15
Griffin, Michael 19

Hope, Chris 19
Houston Texans 20
Huff, Michael 20
Hutson, Don 8

Indianapolis Colts 38

Johnson, Andre 20

Krause, Paul 12

Lane, Dick "Night Train" 11
Los Angeles Rams 11, 15
Lott, Ronnie 13, 35
Luckman, Sid 7

Manning, Peyton 38
McNabb, Donovan 31
Minnesota Vikings 12, 22, 34

New England Patriots 18, 37
Newman, Terence 24, 32
New York Giants 10
New York Jets 18

Oakland Raiders 20, 26, 28

Philadelphia Eagles 31, 37, 39
Pittsburgh Steelers 4, 5, 12, 14, 23, 35
Polamalu, Troy 4, 5, 23, 35
Portis, Clinton 36

Reed, Ed 39
Revis, Darrelle 19

St. Louis Cardinals 31
Samuel, Asante 37
Sanders, Bob 38
Sanders, Deion 20
San Diego Chargers 25
San Francisco 49ers 13
Sharper, Darren 34
Slater, Jackie 15
Smith, Steve 21, 26

Tampa Bay Buccaneers 29
Tennessee Titans 19
Tunnell, Emlen 10

Washington Redskins 9, 12, 15, 36
Welker, Wes 18
Wilson, Adrian 31
Winfield, Antoine 22
Woodson, Charles 30
Woodson, Rod 14

About the Author

Jim Gigliotti is a freelance writer who lives in southern California with his wife and two children. A former editor at NFL Publishing, he has written more than two dozen books for youngsters and adults, including *Stadium Stories: USC Trojans* and kids' titles on football stars Tom Brady, Peyton Manning, and LaDainian Tomlinson.